A Year in the

BIG SOUTH FORK

NATIONAL RIVER AND RECREATION AREA

Photographs and Text by Chuck Summers

Foreword by Howard Baker, Jr.

To David and Ava Laxton
for their generous support of
my photographic endeavors
and their uncompromising
commitment to the preservation
of the Big South Fork National
River and Recreation Area.

A Year in the Big South Fork
National River and Recreation Area
By Chuck Summers

ISBN 0-9668525-0-8

Printed in Hong Kong.
First printing, Winter 1999.

PRODUCTION MANAGEMENT:
Mount Pleasant Productions,
P.O. Box 955, Port Angeles, WA 98362
DESIGN AND TYPOGRAPHY: Elizabeth Watson
COPY EDITING: Kate Reavey

Front cover: East Rim Overlook view.
Page 1: Coneflower.
Page 2: Big South Fork entrance.
Page 3: Leatherwood Ford reflections.
Page 4: Angel Falls Overlook.
Page 6: Eastern redbud and dogwood.
Page 46: View from East Rim Overlook.
Page 47: Cardinal.
Page 48: Rhododendron.
Back cover: Leatherwood Ford reflections,
and Virginia bluebells.

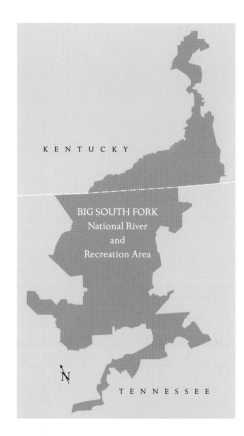

KENTUCKY

BIG SOUTH FORK
National River
and
Recreation Area

N

TENNESSEE

P r e f a c e

Photographers from William Henry Jackson to Ansel Adams have had a love affair with the landscapes within America's National Parks. Chuck Summers' images of the Big South Fork National River and Recreation Area continue a tradition of bringing the richness of our parks to the public through the medium of photography. This beautiful book invites readers to savor the Big South Fork's natural resources. I hope the images and words will inspire you to visit the park often and to experience its remarkable seasonal transitions.

Rolland R. Swain, *Superintendent*
Big South Fork National River and Recreation Area

Foreword

The Big South Fork National River and Recreation Area straddles Tennessee and Kentucky, covering over 106,000 acres of federally protected land. I am proud to be a native of Scott County, Tennessee, located in this region, and to have been the principal sponsor of the enabling legislation that created this park in 1974. I am a frequent visitor to the Big South Fork National River and Recreation Area, primarily in pursuit of its many opportunities to practice my favorite hobby of photography. But opportunity is available for many other pursuits as well—horseback riding, hunting, fishing, hiking, canoeing, rafting, mountain biking, rappelling, camping, and the list goes on and on.

This region so rich in natural beauty is also rich in its people. People of an independent and hard working spirit who continue to demonstrate the qualities that made settling this difficult and rocky terrain possible. People with an independent nature so strong that when Tennessee seceded from the Union during the period of the Civil War, Scott County seceded from the State of Tennessee and briefly became the Independent State of Scott.

It is reported that the Cumberlands were the first mountains that John Muir ever saw, and it was in Tennessee in 1867 that the future founder of the Sierra Club decided to commit himself to a life of environmental activism. Here conservatism may be at its most profound, but it is a personal rather than an ideological conservatism, the traditional kind that springs from a genuine celebration of the world as it is, the kind that keeps people close to the earth and rejoices in life's simplest pleasures.

Chuck Summers is a talented photographer who lets us share the beauty of some of life's most outstanding simple pleasures. He takes us on a year long tour of the Big South Fork—one of this nation's great hidden treasures. He allows us to experience the changing seasons through his lens and the opportunity to contemplate how this all came to be.

I've often referred to this part of the country as the "Center of the Universe"—take a couple of trips through this book and you'll begin to understand why.

Howard H. Baker, Jr.
Huntsville, Tennessee

Introduction

The great conservationist John Muir once said everyone needs "places to play in and pray in where nature may heal and cheer and give strength to body and soul alike." The Big South Fork National River and Recreation Area is such a place. It is a place of great and subtle natural beauty, where I can walk quietly along the forested trails to reach high rock promontories or to find rest and contemplation in the company of Virginia bluebells on the cool banks of the river. The sandstone arches and outcroppings formed over millennia have so amazed me that I return again and again to photograph them, as their moods change with time, with the powers of wind and water, and with the changing light of each new season.

Traversed by the Big South Fork of the Cumberland River, this is a park rich with diverse habitats, weaving a complex fabric of flora and fauna across ancient sandstone. The Big South Fork draws nearly a million visitors each year. Still, it takes only a short walk to find solitude in the company of wildflowers, lichen, and river song. Access to this solitude is one of the park's greatest attributes and is the central reason I return: to find myself immersed in the beauty of creation.

For the past ten years, I have been privileged to live near the Big South Fork. This proximity has provided opportunities for planned and spontaneous travel to the park, where I once again connect with the natural world and focus my eyes, my heart, and finally my camera lens on the unique splendor of the changing seasons in the Big South Fork.

Each season has its unique sensory gifts. From the brilliant colors of the first spring wildflowers, to the power of river rapids after a summer thundershower, to the sweet smells of the forest floor in autumn, each seasonal change is dear to my heart. Finally, the cold of the shaded winter forests and the white stillness of snow remind us that rest, too, is essential, and that spring's renewal can't be far behind.

I invite you, through the images in this book, to explore a year in the Big South Fork, a place for which I hold great reverence. My wish is that you have the opportunity to visit this place, to personally experience its inspirational powers, and to discover, like John Muir, that interaction with nature gives "strength to the body and soul alike."

Chuck Summers, *Autumn 1998*

▶ *The sandy soil deposited along*
the banks of the park's rivers provides the
ideal habitat for these Virginia bluebells.
▶ ▶ *A member of the Orchid family,*
the yellow lady slipper is one of the most
popular wildflowers in the park.
Two varieties grow within
the Big South Fork.

SPRING

Spring comes slowly to the Big South Fork. Winter weather can linger into the end of March and through the first weeks of April. My spirit is stirred with the first signs of spring blooming across the forest floor: bloodroot, spring beauty, and trout lilies emerging from the carpet of decomposing leaves. Deciduous trees unravel delicate green new growth. Redbuds infuse the landscape with vibrant magenta, then the soft white blossoms of the dogwood appear. Spring rain showers funnel into the creeks and tributaries of the Big South Fork of the Cumberland River, turning trickles into steep waterfalls that dance with mist and small rainbows. The migratory return of the whip-poor-will and woodthrush from their southern habitats, the terrestrial movement of reptiles and amphibians, the birth of the year's fawns, and, at night, the sounds of peepers confirm that the equinox has arrived. This is the time of return and renewal, when nature displays its regenerative powers and the wonders of creation become a source of inspiration for any who will watch and listen.

Perhaps spring does not actually come slowly to the Big South Fork. Like a child eagerly awaiting a special event, I am restless after the long winter and only perceive that time is passing slowly. For when spring does arrive, it is robust with the colorful proliferation of new life. Longer days illuminate the landscape with a special quality of vernal light, urging me to rise early, walk the trails, and discover the familiar blossoms and sudden waterfalls of the coming day.

▲ *Jack-in-the-pulpit, a member of the Arum family, will produce brilliant clusters of red berries in the fall.*
◄ *The cinnamon fern thrives in wet woods and marshes. The brown fertile fronds have a cinnamon-like appearance, hence the name.*

In spring, whitetail deer give birth to spotted fawns,
naturally camouflaged for their protection.

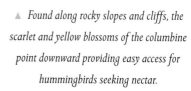

▲ *Found along rocky slopes and cliffs, the scarlet and yellow blossoms of the columbine point downward providing easy access for hummingbirds seeking nectar.*

◄ *A foggy morning on the Clear Fork River. The Clear Fork and New Rivers eventually join to form the Big South Fork of the Cumberland River.*

▶ *Yahoo Falls, located in the northern extremities of the park, is the highest waterfall in Kentucky. It has a vertical drop of approximately 113 feet and descends in front of a large rock shelter.*

▼ *The speckled leaves of the trout lily are said to resemble the pattern found on trout.*

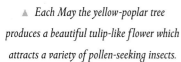

▲ *Each May the yellow-poplar tree produces a beautiful tulip-like flower which attracts a variety of pollen-seeking insects.*

◄ *Accessible by car, Honey Creek Overlook offers one of the most outstanding views in the Big South Fork. Here one may view the sandstone walls which forced the river to move downward, creating a gorge several hundred feet deep.*

► *Several ponds dot the landscape of the Big South Fork. These provide important habitat for a variety of wildlife. Many of these ponds are remnants of homesteads and farms present before the creation of the park.*

◄ *Thriving in acidic soil, mountain laurel is abundant in the southern Appalachians. This evergreen shrub produces a cluster of delicate saucer-shaped flowers ranging in color from deep pink to white.*

▼ *Showy orchis appear in the shade of the woods throughout the park. Three to twelve purple and white flowers bloom annually on a terminal spike.*

▲ *Heavily logged earlier this century, the Big South Fork's second growth forests*
provide evidence of nature's regenerative powers.

SUMMER

▶ *A female Diana turns
to a thistle for nourishment. Butterflies
are cold-blooded and as a result are
most active on sunny warm days.*
▶ ▶ *Heal-all, once thought to be
a cure for many ailments, adds a
touch of color to the fields of
the Big South Fork.*

SUMMER

Hazy, hot, and humid are the words that I hear most commonly used to describe summer in the Big South Fork. While humans tend to retreat to air conditioned enclosures, most species thrive in these conditions. Peering down from one of the park's numerous overlooks, I am impressed by the density of the darker green forest canopy and its vivid contrast with the lighter and vari-colored greens of spring. Photosynthesis is profusely active here and the forests literally breathe oxygen into the ecosystem. Summer blossoms, including the coneflower and goldenrod, add surges of color to their surroundings, but it is the composite of lovely, darker green gradations which dominate the landscape.

Vociferous crickets, katydids, bullfrogs, and a cadre of kindred spirits perform daily cacophonies that carry with them fond memories of summers past. This is the music of the Big South Fork, reason enough to be a summer traveler here. Summer light brings long, delightful days, so that there never seems to be enough time to enjoy all the wonders of the season.

▲ *A century ago, the American chestnut was prolific across southern forests,*
yielding nearly half of the region's mast crop. A blight has now eliminated the towering
American chestnut and only non-native species like this Chinese chestnut remain.
▶ *The South Arch has a span of 135 feet and a clearance of 70 feet.*

◄ *Devil's Cave is one of*
many geologic features found
off the beaten path.
▼ *Mushrooms enjoy a symbiotic*
relationship with other living plants,
providing and receiving
nourishment from one another.

Many small streams drain the hillsides of the Big South Fork area.
In drier seasons these are reduced to bare trickles.

◀ *The boulder-strewn area near Blue Heron, known as Devil's Jump, is the last significant rapid before the river leaves the park. Blue Heron was once the site of a vital coal mining community.*

▼ *Absent from the region for nearly a century, black bears have been moved to the Big South Fork from the Great Smoky Mountains National Park as part of an experimental plan.*

▲ *A sulphur butterfly*
helps provide pollination for the
brilliant red cardinal flower.
▶ *A commanding view of*
the Station Camp and Charit Creek
drainages is available atop the
South Arch of the Twin Arches.
An easy .7-mile trail leads
to this popular area.

▲ *Goldenrod and ironweed are considered nothing more than weeds by many. This vibrant display, found behind the Park Headquarters, shows the genuine beauty of these misunderstood wildflowers.*

▲ *The eastern cottontail is the
most common rabbit in North America.
Cottontails produce 3-4 litters
per year of 1-9 young.*

▶ *As the sun begins to set,
the sandstone bluffs in the O & W
Bridge area begin to glow in warm light.
Turkey vultures often soar above
these imposing bluffs.*

AUTUMN

▶ *The orange husks of the*
American bittersweet burst open each
fall to reveal the bright red seeds within.
The fruit produced by these twining
vines is not edible.

▶ ▶ *One of many species of owls*
within the park, the barn owl is
a nocturnal hunter who requires
only its ears to locate and capture
its small-mammal prey.

AUTUMN

Magic and wonder, color and light: this is autumn in the Big South Fork. The park's expansive forest of hardwood trees are alight with rich hues that rival those of New England. Cooler nights help to create a marvelous atmospheric condition so that a certain low-lying morning fog comes to define the river corridor. As this fog begins to sift up the short side valleys, the colorful forested ridges seem to float above a mystical scene alive with the changes of temperature and light that only autumn can bring.

The sun swings farther to the south with each passing day, and daylight wanes, giving way to cool temperatures and sometimes strong winds. Leaves are carried to the forest floor, where they will become soil in due time. As I witness these floating, spiraling leaves, the days become more quiet in the Big South Fork. Birds have migrated, hibernating animals burrow in, leaves come to rest on the forest floor. Autumn brings with it a distinct feeling of closure, and I know that winter cannot be far behind.

▲ *In autumn, pine cones and*
colorful leaves litter the forest floor,
enriching the soil as their nutrients
are recycled in nature's economy.
◀ *Rugged and steep cliffs,*
along with cavernous rock shelters,
seem to epitomize the Big South Fork.
For centuries rock shelters have
provided protection for humans
and animals alike.

The many different species of hardwood trees display a stunning palette of color each fall. Maples, oaks, hickories, dogwoods, sweetgums, and all the others add distinctive colors to the mix.

▲ *The Big South Fork of the Cumberland River begins in Tennessee and flows north into Kentucky.*
During autumn, shallow pools reflect the beautiful colors of the nearby forest.

▶ *Cool autumn nights contribute*
to the low lying fogs that follow
the path of the river. Below East Rim
Overlook, colorful islands appear
to float above the fog.

◄ *Dewdrops outline the web of this orb weaver spider. Spiders have eight legs and belong to a group called arachnids.*

► *Red maple is the most common maple in the park. The red pigments in the leaves dominate in autumn once the tree ceases to produce chlorophyll.*

◄ The Twin Arches are thought to have held sacred significance for Native Americans who lived in this area centuries ago. The arches continue to be a source of inspiration to park visitors.

▼ Following autumn rains, mushrooms begin to grow at a rapid pace. An amazing variety grow within the park.

▲ *Scientists know how leaves change color but not why. Many visitors return*
year after year simply to enjoy the unexplained beauty of the colorful displays.

WINTER

▶ *The American beech is one*
of the last trees to release its leaves
each year. The tree produces beechnuts
which provide sustenance for
mammals large and small.
▶ ▶ *Whitetail bucks shed their*
antlers each winter. A new set will
begin to emerge come spring.

WINTER

Winter is characterized by stillness and quiet. Gentle rain and gray skies prevail. The deciduous trees are leafless, except for a few beeches which remain sporadically ornamented by brownish orange leaves. Evergreen trees (hemlocks, pine, and cedar), shrubs (rhododendron and mountain laurel), and some lingering berries also add touches of color to the quiescent, monochromatic landscape.

The visual mood is subdued, until the first heavy freeze brings with it a geometry of icicles and hoarfrost. Although winter weather in the Big South Fork is unpredictable and heavy snowfall rare, when significant storms do occur, they bring with them the austere contrasts that mark this stark season. I am drawn to such contrasts, especially the patterns and shapes of trees, which are now, as in no other season, silhouettes. These hardwoods stand tall against a backdrop of white, their bare limbs an elegant reminder of the abundant colors the forest held in early autumn.

In this pure white cover, with its dark silhouettes, the land seems to sleep, readying itself for the coming light. My spirit, too, can rest, as the days slowly expand and winter gives way to the eternal vibrancy of spring.

▲ *The bright berries of the*
American holly are a favorite food
source for many song and game birds.
◀ *Situated next to the road leading*
to the Bear Creek Overlook, Split Bow
Arch is one of the most accessible and
interesting arches in the park.

▲ *Ice bells form on river boulders when the temperature plummets below freezing.*

Due to the area's relatively mild winters, the river itself seldom freezes.

▲ *The beauty of the Big South Fork region is made manifest at its many overlooks.*

An easy .1-mile trail leads to the East Rim Overlook, offering this view of the river far below.

▶ *Despite frigid temperatures,*
runoff behind Yahoo Falls
pushes on to the river a
short distance away.

◄ *A late winter snow covers*
the rocks lining the river below the O & W
Bridge. Snow serves the useful purpose
of insulating plants and hibernating
animals from the cold.

▶ *Icicles form on rhododendron*
branches and leaves. Their leaves
curl up in freezing weather,
enabling them to survive
winter's chill.

Suggested Reading

Nature Through The Seasons. Richard Adams. Simon & Schuster, 1975.

Big South Fork Country. Howard Baker and John Netherton. Rutledge Hill Press, 1993.

The Field Guide to Wildlife Habitats of the Eastern United States. Janine M. Benyus. Simon & Schuster, 1989.

Hollows, Peepers, and Highlanders: An Appalachian Mountain Ecology. George Constantz. Mountain Press, 1994.

Listening to Nature: How to Deepen Your Awareness of Nature. Joseph Cornell. Dawn Publications, 1987.

Hiking the Big South Fork. Brenda Deaver, Jo Anna Smith and Howard Ray Duncan. Third Edition. University of Tennessee Press, 1999.

The Book of Forest and Thicket: Trees, Shrubs, and Wildflowers of Eastern North America. Stackpole Books, 1992.

A Field Guide to Eastern Forests. Peterson Field Guides, John C. Kricher and Gordon Morrison. Houghton Mifflin Company, 1988.

Mountain Year: A Southern Appalachian Nature Notebook. Barbara G. Hallowell. John F. Blair, Publisher, 1998.

The Smithsonian Guides to Natural America: Central Appalachia. Bruce Hopkins. Random House, 1996.

Exploring the Big South Fork: A Handbook to the National River and Recreation Area. Russ Manning. Mountain Laurel Place, 1994.

The Historic Cumberland Plateau: An Explorer's Guide. Russ Manning. University of Tennessee Press, 1993.

Trails of the Big South Fork. Russ Manning and Sondra Jamieson. Third Edition. Mountain Laurel Place, 1995.

Seasonal Guide to the Natural Year: North Carolina, South Carolina, Tennessee. John Rucker. Fulcrum Publishing, 1996.

Eastern Forests. The Audubon Society Nature Guides. Ann Sutton and Myron Sutton. Alfred A. Knopf, 1988.

Forests: A Naturalist's Guide to Trees and Forest Ecology. Laurence C. Walker. John Wiley & Sons, Inc., 1990

A c k n o w l e d g m e n t s

The publication of this book serves as a personal reminder of my indebtedness to many people. I feel especially blessed to have had my mentor and friend, Pat O'Hara, produce my first book. Pat's exquisite photography has been a source of inspiration to me for many years. I am also very grateful for the support of Rolland Swain and the staff at the Big South Fork National River and Recreation Area. In particular, park rangers Ron Wilson and Howard Ray Duncan have gone out of their way to assist me. I am likewise indebted to Howard Baker, Jr. for providing the foreword to this book. It is a great honor to have him associated with this work. In addition to these I would like to thank Ken Jenkins and Bill Fortney for their support and encouragement. Both have helped me become a better photographer. I offer special thanks to the good people at Wilderness Resorts, who have provided me with lovely cabin accommodations during my visits to the park. My gratitude for the love and support of my wife, Bonita, family, friends, and church along the way cannot be adequately expressed. Finally, I want to thank my heavenly Father for the beauty of His creation and the gift of His Son. I have been truly blessed beyond measure.

For information about the park contact:
Big South Fork National River
    and Recreation Area,
4564 Leatherwood Road,
Oneida, Tennessee 37841, (931)879-3625
@www.NPS.GOV/BISO/INDEX.htm

Those interested in supporting the Friends of the Big South Fork National River and Recreation Area may call (423)569-1599, or write Friends of the Big South Fork, P.O. Box 5407, Oneida, TN 37841.

The author would like to thank Eastern National for their support. Eastern National provides quality educational products and services to America's national parks and other public trusts. Eastern National can be reached at 470 Maryland Drive, Suite 1, Fort Washington, PA. 19034.

Publication of this book was made possible by a grant from Wilderness Resorts, 1463 Big Ridge Road, Oneida, TN 37841, (423)569-9847, www.WILDERNESSRESORTS.com

Fine art editions of the pictures in this book, along with a poster featuring the image on page 33, are available for sale. Those interested in purchasing a print or poster may contact Chuck Summers by writing to Contemplative Images, P.O. Box 324, Jellico, TN, 37762.